DON'T FORGET to BREATHE

Andrew Levy

chax press 2012

ISBN 978 0925904 67 6

Published by Chax Press
411 N 7th Ave Ste 103
Tucson, Arizona 85705-8388
USA

Printed in the United States of America

Contents

To

Heretical citizens
Who possess the mental
Capacity to channel the absurdities
Spewing forth
From capital

Language is a very difficult thing to put into words.

– Voltaire

Billy Dale Shoots to Kill

Give me the abomination no one gets hurt

All that's left, he said, is to grow some skin

Skin grows one millimeter a week
Will you be my f#ckFriend?

What a proposition

Not till he tells me where the abomination is

1. Oprah Winfrey
2. Bob Woodruff
3. Emma Thompson
4. Chipotle offering
5. Hamas

Is the thesis implied in the methodological concept?

Now he tells me where abomination is

Not to force the issue

The trees today, the air

The homespun wood and fry
ring his poop in chips

No one says what they're really doing

If you take this path the level of correlation
Is startling

Take this path, on the other hand

This kind is better

Coarser

The cats and the dogs go in the car

Are there no more wipes in the house?

I'll give you a verbal

I'm using a different book

1, 2, 3 get in line

No deal

Sometimes deals are too dealy

You disturb everybody

Everything is fine

No, we won

No, we won

This is a winning partner race

Back in line

It seems the poor
Are more than welcome
To stay
Are you sure mine is the home for you?

I'd be honored to stay here
Nothing lasts forever

There's no where for me to go

Home, of course
Why didn't I think of it before?
We must work quickly

It turned out very nicely, indeed

It's perfect

The kind of place you ought to run to

But where's the door?

Where exactly is elsewhere?

There is something I must tell you

There's no running
away from them

I tracked them down
Brought them back
Sound and safe

Critical big character seemed limitless

There's a lot of discontent

Their majority is at stake here
They're going to strike out in their own direction

Everyone step forward

It just sounded like nonsense
To me

We have come to take revolutionary action
Against you

Poetry allows the reader

To enter with poetry
A farfetched and difficult end

I had been unfair to poetry my entire life

Playing goalie
Crashing in on the next century

I'm not done

What are your favorite kinds of people?

Sorry, bye

Correcting mistaken ideas
is not my idea

We'll end up in misery

I'm ready willing and able to be your F#ckFriend

I can't decide if you think
I'm a fool

With every piece of flesh I ate, I remembered

They always pretend to try to *pin me down*,
get me to *be precise*. That's the pretense but the truth of it
is that they're threatened

I have an invisible thing, you can't see it

It has such sweetness written
All over it

Fatter Submarine, Longschlong, Girthy Woody, Massive Scallywag
Kick off National Day of Conscience

A masquerade of rage and revanchism

Jam a spoke in the wheel

A false loyalty, if I say I will shut up
I cannot

Am I only what I know of myself?

I recently became a member of a Cyber café and started to
exchange daily e-mails with an American

Get in bed or I'm going to put your lobster away

My pen is all my friends
My pen is karma

Please do not hesitate to contact it

America forever and ever
is an accumulation incorporated
over the weekends of isolated portions
commended either for fragrance
or form
whatever severity of the fantastic
fastidiousness
beneath an uncouth and grotesque
embodiment hallelujah

It'll never be free

I want to investigate the newest techniques and applications for energy-conscious poetics from the superficial page design, down to the quantum physical level

Create desolation
And call it peace

Thinking in the inverted pyramid

Oh go on, you're making me cum
A deux ex machina of cheap, overdone

I don't sound out the silence the same way

I don't know if you are coming, but if you are

But it seems that this was only a metaphor

I don't know where to begin

I'll begin with its meta-historical naïveté, its professionalism

Melodramas are characteristically
written in this way

If you have the time I really need a long-hard-screw

What would our superiors think?

If we can't have sex with little boys
And we are not allowed to have sex with women,
Then we'd have no sex at all

I fully support taking the piss out of pretty much everything

It's almost impossible to put feelings into words

Everybody seems to be imprisoned

Best made for one true purpose – woof!

Woof! Woof!

Let's gettogether andscrew ourbrains outsoon

Cognitive opportunities
For sloth and escape
Will affect
Lame attempts at uniformity

Dying stars eject matter
And may have multiple outflows

In New York City
The dying central star is floating
In a blue haze of hot gas

This corridor of no

If one thinks in a compartmentalized fashion
If one awakes slippery and without name
If one gathers the honey of the dismembered

The light of alcohol, the grapes
And ambient atmosphere

Already in office the Manchurian
Does not ask questions during briefings

Assures the soon-to-be-battered:
"We are fully prepared."

But the rest is fine

Dying stars eject matter

The power that I have is roughly equivalent to that of a lipstick
But the poem with its terrible kisses?

As if it were piss
As if was osmosis
As if were possible to do anything with them

Do you think it knows what we're talking about, said Smithy?
Didn't you have to promise, a hundred times…?

NO
It germinates, an Almond Joy stuck on one's palette

Heinrich says (while studiously avoiding them) their dogs
Are wearing them down – the verse cannot keep it fixed

The lovely black and white is flying back

Put your name
With theirs

Sign this

It comes out of thin air

It is easy to feel that if Levy had written in English,
he would have written in this English

Multiple outflows

I don't feel safe in my own bedroom –
or in the whole country

Anne Raggedy emails: ride me please

Life is unfair

Let's pick up the pieces, in theory

At high speeds along a preferred axis

Fiscal peace of mind as genre
English is 3 years old

We know so much
It takes great discipline and effort
To hear each other

Exceptions to rules?

People deserve them, right?

Let me take this table out of your way

It's better to play

Without this table
in the way

I don't care if you're a grownup, and I'm not

I don't care

Would you like being forced into a whole other person?

Then you turn into a show-off
I mean it

How would you like it if a man walked up to you and said,
"Would you like someone who could turn you
into a whole new different person?"

And he did

Would you like that?

Give us a choice
Of what motivates the not true

Her English is 6 years old

An anomaly in an ocean of Nirvana

Okay, to be clear. You are saying that there is a written policy
that excludes the _______ in such decisions

I would like to see that text

World gets 102 more billionaires
A record 793, up 102 from last year

You may
bring
a calculator

I'm a classicist, so I naturally prefer the devil

The devil's in the detail

But you might like the lurid color and lurid plotting

Your call

They felt I was positive and had optimistic views

They vote with their pocketbooks
They vote with the books that have emptied their pocketbooks

I never wanted to be famous,
especially not in this way

The situation turns both nasty and grimly hilarious

Would you be available a lot for sex?
I could really use a fuck friend

Numa Reunião, numa Aula,
num Tribunal, numa Conferência,
num Palco, numa Tribuna,
por exemplo?

Hope to see you at tonight's Megillah reading

Give us a choice
Of what motivates the not true

A full tank of gasoline
Hard facts
I thought
To spread my seeing

Imagined the feeling of holding the money
In my hands that I would make myself
For the first time

I always let you do everything

The truth is not what you are thinking

I haven't seen it in an American since 1927

I want to be a mermaid
With orange hair

My name is Sophocles

It's called
You Guess

I am the author of Oedipus Rex

In the land of make-believe
I want all of it

You're going to soak in the tub 15-minutes

Keep your mouth shut, and blow

Does retirement have to wait
until 90?

What is this with the clothing line?

It's just another way we can deliver education

I'm a great believer
In education

It needs acquiescence

A *demand* for intelligence?

I'm 178 years old, but I want to go fast

You say we shouldn't have to be *here*
But we are

I say we shouldn't have to be free
And that whenever we deny it,
we want it

I spend my whole life
Cleaning up *our* stuff

It's a feeling of suspense
I'm a super hero

The poem did not have to be perfect

Perfections delivery – Does it depend
upon the personality of the reader?

People fall from earth
It is understandable
that they do so for their
generosity

It might be black and or
white but you could
theoretically read poems
on the poet itself

You'll harvest what you grow
So plant things in a row

There is no iron-clad guarantee
I'm losing my mind

If there really *is* something

A full tank of gasoline
Hard facts

Trapped in that horrific cage

Beaten down, dirty
Ready to complain

I can't even think about other boys

You've proved to me that I do have a value
Just like very berry

You can call me Nothing
Which is Something

If you stay right where you are, I won't see you

The president is dead
Wrong

"Always keep your words sweet.
You never know when you will have to eat them."
Joseph Aidala

Deadly weather...

It appeared to consist of
variously sized corporate and residential "islands" distributed over what I
imagine was once open prairie, and then later an immense cattle range,
interconnected by multiple overpasses and highways

The ball that comes closest wins

Hey, you can't knock my ball away...
That's cheating!

Haven't you ever seen a wishing-well before?

It sure is beautiful, Bernadette

Maybe your feathers
Will help to inspire me
To finish my poem

Would you like one, Bob?

I'm trying to make myself more colorful

No one's behaving nicely

The travel industry's purloined icon is melting

Your color helps you blend in with your surroundings
And keeps you safe

Especially when you hang upside-down
And don't move

I think you're a real natural in the
Poetry department, Bob

Your words do paint a picture

The millennial snowcap that was said to cover
King Solomon's tomb is receding

I love being friends, don't you?

Now where is… Harry?

My nose likes Harry

You'll find me hanging
Upside-down

This small world
Is
Yours and mine

Hey… it's me, Snook

I wonder what smells Bob likes best?
But it seems that this was only a metaphor

I don't know where to begin

Lala lala lala la la-la-la…
Lala lala lala la la-la-la…

No one wants civil war

Huh?

It's so bad, it looks like
The wrath of god

Who, what, where

Oedipus the kind

Could you be an owner, and I'll be
An employee?

Can you play with us?

What art should be:
Unconscious, ideal, and remote?

E-mail dot article
printers
mere over dot underwear
nieuwsbrieven

suture me mail over
Utile   Beware

Life without poems… I'll break it down

The capital that I have
Is not youth
or financial backing

Now it's all gone

So I could open the presents?

I've got a different one for you…

You are forgetting that I am your superior!

Do you know where she is?

A wooden utensil
Your incompetence
Can be made useful
As ornament

They say you're beautiful

No time to enjoy
It's time we stood up
To the scenery

I want this to be an unforgettable show

A display of my absolute
Power

You've broken all of the evil enchantments

None of this would be possible
Without you

I like the teeth

I'm going to be right back

What's next, a singing
Donut?

Trust me my pungent friend

You've got to start
All over again

There is no further negotiation
Possible

We've got a dislocated
Schedule

Our fighting has become a tool
To build their wealth

Gwyneth welcomes baby Moses

Most of these folks just won't allow
for discussions that aren't grounded
in a very specific reading of material reality,
which presumably "explains" not only
Who We Are
but
Who We Imagine Ourselves To Be...

Picture Dorian Gray
In the land of discovery

"You must like my nose"

"How much does it cost?"

Love isn't all you need

What are you?
And who are you doing?

Everybody seems to have a great idea
But for me

It's being there

It's not what you bring

It's like…

You don't want to be late to heaven

A pen chants for innocent yet compelling permanent identity

Here and there,
Nowhere gradually inches into
Conversationalism, greed, contradictions
Of inefficiency

And you can chat with them
And be glad you did

"occasion-stained lyrics"
Or bad writing?

One can build a snowman if one likes

I love snow

We can have lots of snow-puppies

Nobody cares where one came from

Everybody wants to find out
What that pup has achieved

You're completely surrounded by my troops

The D.I. is one fucking hard ass Marine
Drill sergeant son of a bitch

We're doomed

What if we split up the remembering?

In selling his house he becomes immortal

His BMWs are turning against him

I'm a person if you ask me questions
You want to know who I am?
I'm a person if you're too inquisitive
I tune you out completely

A steroidal view
In the forest of error

Plan crashed into World Tread Center

His BMs
Are turning against him

This all depends on which direction
The wind blows

People always make smells
Into big stories

"Two tombs up!"

The white choice of action

That's so deep
The world can't stand it

It's Elmo upside down
Swinging in a tree

I want some dust please

I need it

I heard such mendacity
Is good for one's soul

I do not cannibalize my friends
But I do eat them

Late at night
There's almost the sense that nothing
Is going on

There's no running away from it

All those slugs that have washed over this soil

I cannot put our lobster

Away within our memory
Their terrible accounting, their terrible
Disastrous theft

To pick up the images out of thin air

The final rescue of all their children
who are in chains

To awaken from the hands of tyrants

To redeem time and event
That I ate that night

The thought of being free

Our moral prejudices?
To air our moral prejudices?

Melting into the grass on Central Park during a gentler moment of parenthood

Get rich in 8 miles

Share the love

You are already way out of your depth on the question
of moral equivalence

Where could I have put that pitchfork?

It's the penis that gets you
It's the biggest one in the world

Just right for barbecues
I'll be able to sit outside on summer
Evenings

I could use a drink after all that work

We live in a real war, everyday

– i.e. an appropriation of fascist iconography
meant to critique fascism, eh?

What?

I'm happy to listen to it

Dumb as cum

Our country stands today, where it stands

If you ran a drug company, what would you change?

It's all for your own protection until
You feel your own reflection

To avoid getting led away in handcuffs – a fate so many politicians deserve
People would work out for themselves what they feel

I would try to prevent it

I would bend over backwards to build good relations with those who don't agree with me

All of my stuff has something in it that says,
Great!

I don't have a particular thing I want to say about life;
just pictures in my head

Moral defectiveness?

Human beings
Everywhere do terrible things
To one another

Poetry allows the reader to enter
With poetry a difficult mine

Leads us off the shortcut

This is probably an illusion

Our ears sight the most excellent
Deficit

The moral price, the aggressiveness
Of attention

As if there were some other mediation
Translated into indecencies

Asking, *what's wrong?*

From pride rock to the pit of shame

Quick, before the hyena come!

I want to live where we don't have to dig tunnels
And stick our heads in the sand

It's nature's design?

Grass intolerant?

All you have to do is watch for hyenas and yell
If you see one

Delicious, organic, not merely food

That *we* do not suffer *enough*
Burns up the referendum, the ignorance

The *where are you going?*

Constant Sorrow

The ceremony of "super-realism"
Is not a protection
To retain the disadvantages
In all countries
Insipid world of minimal beliefs
One caricature
An amalgam of apocalyptic devils
Dustbins, indiscriminate pity

Beauty embodied in a small piece
Of paper—or a word, the conjunction
Almond of a mere vessel, your own
Poverty, faithless feet
Cell phones, the tree in front of me
Very simply, very clearly
The handsome indicative nuclear
Perishment

Pose a poem or surprise
Political homelessness or homily repeated
Disembodied point—the psalm, or
Passage put in its place
This love-in-the-air? Something
Thought? – Gossamer love of the language
Between the heated and the cool?
Repudiation? Protocol?

A sign of strength, contact all fours
Jump backwards
Providers of deception privilege
Easily deceived and prosperous
Dismantling the disappointed
Blanketing or lack thereof pointing to
A new UN resolution – Indonesian
Osama bin Laden McChicken

Through the plains of importance
George of the Jungle running full force
The chief support of his house
And utmost purity of heart
Elevated and magnified and dodging to persuade
Meaning nothing and that
Everything noticeable is spurious

Somnolence tortured exempts
Conflicts "self-elf" or "shelf-exemption"
The national idiom suppressed by
The other possibility, the country
Interrupted in its perplexed
Pillars of law perpetuates the riskless
Although technically yearned toward
Doesn't that make sense?

That's our stroller; do you want it?
Pretend it's diabolical, delicious, and organic
Not merely food all bodies apprehended
What regardless of origin or intention
Is obvious about Heads of State
A strange sense of yearning and tact
The self-appointed
Possessed and turning inside out

Defer to the wind or the rain?
No lyric interference will make them
Their bodies in partial or majority
Ownership transmit one place to another
People getting a hard-on
Will carry conviction with them
Financially and emotionally
The oxygen's going to be sucked out

To swing, or not to swing?
Let's keep it on a schedule, then Daddy
Will come in …
Can I just tell you something?
Networks that relay billions of trades
At breathtaking velocities
Draw profits from future production
I'm going to blow up

I'll give you a gerbil

I'm using a different look

1, 2, 3 from this day forth

Whatever such a mind sees in a flower

To eco the atomic bomb—offers them
Little touches of emancipation

When) I see extreme reactions
Because) he is permanently bodiless
Cultural cultures homogenized
For their interpreta-tations
Identify a number of serious problems
For example, how the hell do we
Get out?! What's the point of being
Bent over every time?

Slavery is dark blue like the sea

Tortures condensed approximation had
Already been lavished upon us

Thought consists of a paper cut
A light cotton dressing

For either practical or sentimental reasons

It's not a protection

I felt stricken with terror every time
Gave a jerk

Every one of us like this servant is
An artifact or object of craft

Out of all the stream of human life
And action

Implicated
Scattered
Intensified
Sovereign

A Good Thing in an Unfortunate Manner 2

There is a wide difference

it's just one cyber-mile long

I've been in this broken place before
who chalked on the floor?

I see you
I know who you are

Ole, Conquistador

Imitate me if you can

Constant Sorrow 2

It angelizes, disembodies
Turns into software

Distant Partisans

Ought to be treated humanely

Religionists are all Catholics too
Out of wedlock

Telephone calls
Routed directly through
The twilight zone

Labour union
Elimination

Even I'm sick of the color purple
And I'm purple

You're very thorough
In each of your attachments

There's something here that speaks
To you directly, saying terrible things
About forces beyond your control,
Lines of intersection that cut through
History and logic and every reason-
Able layer of human expectation

He wondered into it
The boy got lost and wandered
Clear-eyed into horror

This is a poem about straying too far

Spirits living apart from their bodies
This is why they're out there

Savage indignation there
Cannot lacerate the breast

Levy has sailed into the rest

Inspiring new ideas
And creativity

In the forest of error
The alternative personhood

Hi,
I'mLooking ForA GuyWho WantsTo GetFreaky WithMe

Zoom in
Above the emotiononationalist circle

Their territorial wood rows
Through the air they breathe

If I am short of breath, and I am
Statues of Liberation through Christ
In their commercial appeal
"Jehovah" inscribed on her crown
The global warming impact of driving a mile
Will double

An intrusion attempt
To be biologically productive
I can hand one or two copies to you
Send me your address
If you'd rather get it in the mail

The wrath of god
Cannot (apparently) lacerate
This breast

Do you want my cell number?

As with all energy conversions, turning words
Into natural poetry or a global rhetoric means losing
Something in translation —

If the cultural difference is big enough the loss is not
Something that translators will worry about

Until someone burps
In Carbon County

Korean sesame skirt steak
Cedar plank salmon

Such 'thin' definitions are another asymmetry
Used to undermine democracy

We love this stuff
Who exactly is 'we'?

You won't be able to try it
If you don't know the secret

Girthy Woody? Massive Scallywag?

... do you like her outfit?

I'm never ever going to change

Which one do you want to be?

How could a flower talk?
How do flowers talk?

Say it!

If I guess wrong and you guess right
Then you win a trophy, right?

All governance might have
The faint aroma of snow

Work it and more comes out?

A Vice-President in charge of Anonymity
Who does what he or she can to keep people
From learning about the writing community's
Good products and good works

All sports are dangerous

You of all people is in a position to be quiet

What are you doing here?
Inside my trousers?

Why can't I get a banana?
You want a banana?

This autonomy
Is verbal nonsense

Are you talking?

I'm not cutting it open yet
There is no war
That could make me

I'm not anorexic

Why *would* you want to face the rest of your life?
(… yet another encapsulating theory)

There is nothing loud enough to hear
I'm sorry, but I'm just not

I like drizzle, it matches
My personality
I'm having trouble steering

There is nothing loud enough to hear

I'm going to teach those girls
A lesson they'll never forget

'We' won't let anyone get hurt

… My fortune telling machine
Its vertical heritage
(Don't forget the freeze machine)
Is finished at last …

We can pretend in the forest of feelings
(It's a fortune telling)

A new friend waits for you
On the other side

I felt more and more immersed
In her "way of thinking"
Due in part to a slightly "anxious"
Beer buzz

The rabbit goes around the tree …
Down the hole … I tied my show …
Shoe … thoughts that stuck out to me …
To laugh at whole-heartedly

Daddy!

Take it easy …
Swim to me

You really were swimming,
all by yourself

First, let's be alive
Then we'll be dead

Give me your heart
You'll see

Identify / Consensus

Baseline
Conditions

Distant
Partisans

Counting
Slips

Notorious
Fiasco

Human
Advantage

Worldly
Beings

Punks
Pump

Official
Culture

Global
Individualism

Village
Mass

Meditative
Alchemy

Original
Self

Undiscriminating
Perplexity

Contemporary
Amateur

Moral
Problem

"Good"
"Bad"

Tushy
Face

First
Amendment

Flat
Shoes

Crash
Helmet

Analytical
Weirdness
Human
Liberty

Words
Ancestry

Errand
Wilderness

Painful
Periods

Grammar
Evanescence

Good sight means seeing what is very small
She is not doing anything but breathing

Imperfect
Perfect

Forget to breathe
Constant sorrow

Eucalyptus
Leaves

No punishing
Lao Tsu

Hopes have been blasted
We have no alternative

We have no amenities
Handcuffed and tortured

Electrically
Mine

Pilgrims
Detonated

Unusually
Blunt

Forensic
Suspects

Slender
Stalk

Cloudless
Sky

Save
Hostos

Buried
Corpses

Bush
Administration

Foreign
Soil

International multinationals tolerate furor
Unacceptable investigators considered taboo

Tearful
Eyes

Televised
Praise:

"You said you wanted to have fun"

Big
Tobacco

Saddam
Optimistic

Breathes
Easier
Unspeakably
Wretched

Merry
Merry be

Facing
Artifice

Can't Win
Bomb

Rotten
Tomatoes

Time
Bomb
Vague
Consultation

Vulgar
Boasting

Decorating
Surrounding

Because I think about the program's legality
It renews its pledge at every turn

The Modern
Ghetto

One country becomes a whole continent
Or the king of erotica

Poetry had gained a lasting reputation
A period of consequences

It glowed like milky mother-of-pearl
Ice blending with drifts of cloud

Yet did not break through the lines
Snowbanks were taking flight

Its weight pressed the bedrock
Leaving you behind

Robbery, a Chapter in Etiquette

My fortune telling machine
Is finished at last

What joy to turn something ugly
Into something lovely

Today is going to be a very special day
No more bad feelings here

Come on in and take a swim
You know what the message is

These pastures of plenty
Must always be free

I ain't got no home
In this world

Any
More

A Holiday from Rules

A life-appreciating empathetic mess

If you were doing your job
The poem wouldn't be wrecked

Pardon my wings –
I'm so flighty

You can't control everything

That's not the way an election is supposed …

Yikes, that's a yodeling yak!

… I'm a real animal

Slapstick humor and pseudo-
Intellectual mumbo jumbo

"Moral waivers"
Melt in your hands

This is a well-trained army

This prevents us from seeing

Don't Forget to Breathe

There is always the danger
The facts will fall and part

Repeat what cannot be altered
Infinite and misunderstood

If I were the pronunciation of my name
The miseries of human life, tension of nothing
The softening of its existence, of yours
Arrested through mute consonants
Omniscient flood distributing a cultivated
Fragrance able to be fairly complementary
Or vernacular or made less arbitrary
In this undefinable sweetness

It says to me – it is you who incorporate
Domestications committed atrocities
Doctrines of isolation, the perfect boring
Controls of irresistible onslaught and slaughter
Betray continuity and visions of speckled fish
Calm and judicious views that housed
All of nature qua cultural whims given and
Completed – it is you who's dead

The perfect boring salutary onslaught
Tension of consonants uncultured but cluttered

Complementary arbitration
Continuity housed it is you
The miseries softened flood it is you
Who misunderstood it is you
In this indefinable mumbo jumbo
This yodeling humor

This tasty loyalty?
This secret and secreted polis?

This innocent yet compelling
Permanence

Punishing Lebanon

The distinction between being and … meaning?

I have no art
I do everything as well as I can

I keep thinking about improvements
Upon these lines all the time

In neighboring metals
A heightening of consciousness
Of oncology, legibility
And three-dimensionality
Terror stricken, the miraculous isolated
Replacements
Much talked of but actually a substitute.
All of these things hang by
A gossamer thread of some kind of love
But what is this some-kind-of-love?
I long for something foreign, some fact
Surrounding living, a recipe
In the absence of anonymity, of background
A complete concentration
In which one would not be able
To read the world

I find these
Beautiful facts

I'm ready for the glitter

You guide my hand

All of this space
Can be safe

That not

We Did It

Now
Do you see the monster?

Here is my magic wand

Put it in the puzzle, por favor
The territorial advancement
Is one thing and its
Realization another – the immediacy
Of where the forms were
Placed – they could starve
But they wouldn't quit
At what point can we withdraw?
Intellectualized light?
Practical conditions only find
An impractical chair
When someone calls me a poet
Hegel's dialectic takes over
Time is something I can pretty much handle
As I please – instead of war
We have art, let me come back to
This thought a little bit later
The essential loneliness I feel at the party
The comforting spectre of it
Our bodies so rarely concede
The growing dominance, the suppression
If that is established a series of rising
Terraces turn to tiles

An illiberal riot
Robbery and assault with precursor
Ingredients – mommy has two heads,
Petrified in all the multiplicity
Bits of crystallized life – the stray ears
Falling on them to establish a claim
Snipping off the cluster by incapacitating
Its author – hoping that America
Gets a bloody nose becomes untenable,
A kind of dossier, the absence of clothing
To reveal the curve of its hip
Become nonexistent – as neither
Close nor distant, an inherent identity
By no means factors
A written policy the forms could cave
Stave off an essential comfort
To be put back in its cage

All of this apace, ready for glitter
A hidden bequest, the empty support
That keeps the ugly together
The pure human fact 2006
Drifting offshore
To the extreme north
The global American welcomes
Its extreme figure
The countenance comes into contact
With the world above
Organ of pure receptivity
Nose and ear
The peaceful public witness

Of impropriety
If it blew up secluding
Dissolution its sweet talks
Busy at school
The abomination kept in bed
That inexplicable unbearable
Immanent banker's life
An inactive absence the disarticulates
Empty all over the planet
A pig that neither presupposes
Or states something concrete
The liver nobody wants to consider
This always trembles
That credentials of hands, feet,
And buttocks
Incomprehensible
Virtually erode the epic solidity
Of the materials at hand
To accommodate or pirate power
Or bitterness
(Which leaves no mark)
Or exodus –
That cannot be untied
It will kill you
If you touch it

An Inconvenient Truth or the Bush Doctrine

An outlaw disinterested in making money
Predisposed to many varieties of violence

Recovers in this notorious fiasco
A renascence of philosophical prestige

They don't want to spoil my fun, do they?
My conscience is dissolved only
By a kind of private shame (i.e. ethics)

Absent presences play their parts
Mounting an attack on behalf of their own practice

Listen to them wend their way, it's crazy
I need something sweet to make it through

Exhausted from hunger or love
I enjoy good talk but will not suffer fools

I sometimes get what they call phantom pain
My brain thinks my candidacy is still there

In the field of artillery revealment and
Concealment comes into contact
Veiled in the nothingness it reveals

A promise is a promise
Go to the break-your-promise jail

Coming after the body no one gets hurt
The purpose for its absence is uncertain

The inconvenient fantasies of the cultured
Show viewership is hard to pin down

A man convicted of keeping his dead mother
In a freezer for years so he could keep collecting her
Social Security checks avoided federal prison

Everything seems very casual
Above life

....

The horror of our world, the need for guidance
Is inconclusive, but to me it looks like beauty

You will continue to take chances
And be glad you did

Secretaries of climate change
Say that everything says something

A President of the United States buggers
And sucks the Mexican border police

A select group is looking to the trees
Many are looking to the past

At the end of November 2005, 18 percent of the contiguous U.S.
Was in moderate to extreme drought, in contrast to 6 percent
At the end of November 2004

This is 19 times the world death toll from SARS
Go to the break-your-promise jail

The European heat wave of August 2003
Claimed at least 35,000 lives

The kind of terrible awesomeness of the
Miscellania of America

Design your own Zen garden
I don't have any center in that sense

Foot-dragging celebrities at the core of any filth
That has sustained the insanity for centuries

One of the most unstable masses on earth
Too deeply felt to deny

....

A stupid longing not to know
Makes us killers

I'd wanted the poem to end sooner than it had
But that fact alone made it more than another poem

You might be encouraging the vicissitudes
To a greater degree than the terms
Of ordinary success call for

Thermohaline circulation already gloating
Cashing in on, they think, the next century

Watch the windows open by themselves
I don't think there's anything genetic about it

An indefatigable pupil and proselytizer
Sooner or later you'll live to regret

"You might as well take a gun and shoot yourself!"
It's kind of telling that he chose to walk

The shotgun used in the killings was never found
I don't particularly care the way it is arranged

"Watermelon, here I come!"
Where does he think he is?

What constitutes professional and ethical behavior?
Who closed this door?

Existence, the source of endless pleasure
Is emptied upon this butchery

Known as the Blue Line

An aimless determinism, persistence
That lies outside the subject

Finding comfort there

I've told them to stop, I've told
Them to withdraw

The outskirts are being occupied

Whether their agencies for death function or not
It is their prolonged crisis to be killed

Their democratic opponents will be
"Rolling the wrong dice"

There is not enough time to
Separate them from the environment

An upside down Mediterranean filled
With as much crude as possible

Weapons of mass destruction that's all we've got

"They don't have a discriminatory mindset"

That nation attracts a minimum of several dozen
Spasms every day

A seaside version of Greenwich Village
Headed in the right direction

Exxon earned $114 million per day
That's $79,000 per minute or $1,300
Per second
[Unintelligible guttural sounds]

And? So what?

You have to be patient and intelligent
It doesn't trip off the tongue

Uniquely qualified to convey this corporate message
This class of durable goods disintegrates immediately

Constantly thrown back into the dilemma
Into the eyes of a deceiver

A country cousin shoots to kill

The Collaborator

Who manipulates, who takes (literally)
Our breath away

With a mind so collected he sees clearly
The impropriety of letting it appear so

No stranger to emergencies he

Throws up any probation he has suffered

An etymology of infinite riches

A consternated ostrich burst on the floor

Men, women, and children
Sleep in sheer terror

One should search in oneself for self-recrimination

The buried
The problem

The punishment
The new

The hidden but unsatisfied constancy
The predictable escalation

This one spot

Yedoma

A type of carbon-rich permafrost
That was flash frozen 40,000 years ago

This is the basic structure I'd like to use:

The choice is yours
You pick it out, I'll help

Not knowing one another
Recently arrived
The contestants to the efficient reduction
Effortlessly stride above poverty
Ecstatic in its freefall

You'll never flow in delicate tableaux

Why not?

As an American taxpayer
Every partition overrun
These words inadequately
Convey my anger

I've Got One More Thing to Tell

Let us condemn our shallowness

Two one, or one three?

As for what Armitage said to the Pakistanis: "I
don't know," Snow said. "This could have been a
classic failure to communicate. I just don't know."

'Be prepared to be bombed. Be prepared to go back to the Stone Age.'

An arrow that missed its target

The year that begins tonight is 5767

In a ritual bath called a mikvah,
A Hebrew word that shares a root with "hope"
The spiritual center

The centrality of the home

We want to be alive

Breaking Cliques

The Dictator Tot says,
"It kind of masturbates my inner aura"

Parents are clueless
They're caught like deer in the headlights

They're playing in an area where they
Don't recognize the consequences

This heart sanctuary
Can't be described

All the parts have such a mutual
Dependence on each other

What a person can do, however, is to return
The semen to repair the brain

A form of ecstatic
Repentance to be swallowed
Within each other

My sympathy goes out to the 95%
Who usc these forms of media responsibly

I think of the girl I love
Who I can never forget

Compassionate Technique

To push the envelope
Of a betrayal of trust

It feels good to confess

"Laura is not me. I am not Laura," the person said at the time
"I'm a writer, I'm not Laura"

Whose verbal body is set
As a trap generalizing music and death
In a repetitive society
Of salaries (in their own voices) that
Avail themselves in salons
Or temples to station themselves
In front of perfection, i.e. people
Of power competing in front of
Dependencies between themselves
And the public demand

The world of time says:
"Your love came from me;
There's no place to get to"

People who do not want to speak provide

A wider field
Of anonymity

A Stinking Slick of Black Sludge

A noxious mélange reminiscent
Of rotten eggs, garlic and petroleum
Near manioc and corn fields

The skin of his 6-month-old son,
Salam, bloomed with blisters, which burst
Into weeping sores all over his body

Hydrogen sulfide is a volatile compound
That smells of rotten eggs, but at high
Concentrations you can no longer smell it
It paralyzes your nervous system

Is very lethal and acts very rapidly

"We do not acknowledge responsibility for the
Dumping of the waste without treating it."

Who in the utmost terrors of conscience
Made a public recantation?

MALE: 30-40 years; dying man, famous crime
Fighter and Rabbi (double bass player/upright

Open to other types

Various malefactors, constant churchgoers,
Who, being at the point of death, expressed
Some satisfaction at the news

Turn the Camera On

I am a 25-F-Single woman from russia
Maybe we chat online?
I have been wanting to send you pictures, is this ok?
Let me know:) kiss

Loyalty?

Would you be loyal
to Ted Bundy?

Rumsfeld is
very loyal
He expects it in return
and rewards it

Sit down in the tub

What constitutes accountability?
The election is 33 days away
Are the republicans seriously
Inside your presence?

Throw your arms around me

Fierce

Paper, paper
Oh, how I love paper!

"You don't want to throw somebody away," he says
"But sometimes you have to"

Multiple pages identify Levy as a close friend and
Personal confidante, who is one of the only members
Of the poetry scene to take any interest in them
A former page himself, Levy offers to mentor pages and
Keep in touch with some of them after they have been
Published, according to interviews

"When they tell me they're hearing voices, I tell them
It's just their conscience talking," Levy says

The wish to alter and avert sexual pleasure

Count to four, over and over

Calm down

"Style, how you use words, how you use
Rhetoric, can end up being a kind of symbol
Of how a whole generation is thinking"

It's a miracle
Anyone makes
Their way

Amish Migrate

To help document the middle class,
Which usually escapes, visitors will soon
Descend into a world of the dead

It began with the
realization of my father's inevitable
Mortality, then everything that
followed upon his death a year ago
April set it in stone

I am increasingly confident that I can act
Without serious consequences

I have no bum at all

There's no justice

I think we'd better take matters
Into our own hands

All the parts have such a mutual
Dependence on each other

His heart cannot be described

Though you endeavor with all the resources
At your disposal to translate its concerns, ideas,
And passion into articulate, commanding, and

Eloquently necessary argumentative prose
Death was going through my mind

If you're not part of a clique,
Forget it

The death of a human being
Its incapacity to reconcile itself to time's end
Its reluctance and shame
Its origin on the lips of
An importance which is not new
The fabrication of corpses above all
From the side of death
The quantity that counts
Proper/improper and internal/external
Disappear (there is nothing to hear)
All comportment and all existence
Inauthentic and factual dominions
Every single detail shut

This does not sound particularly esoteric
I know that I've always known it

Who is it?
Say again?

Green pasture to replace small house
For closure

Everything outside it true

Natural Gas

I love pretzels

Oh, sorry
That was a big one

We're over here

No we're not, we're over here

It's just a game
Don't get mad

Nope

What makes you so angry?

When I get mad, I get sooo mad!

I don't need help
I'm big

No fair

I'm always last
And I'm always falling down

Now what?!

Hey, I Can't See

The
U.S. death rate and
Overall toll still
Remain far lower
Than in the Vietnam
War, when 58,000
U.S. troops were
Killed

What does 3 plus 3 make?

Do you think it could be higher?

Two of the victims
Had their throats
Cut and two others
Had been shot

Difficult data

The survey / participants attributed / about 31
percent / of violent deaths to / coalition forces

Come on, I'll help you

Let Me See

Please, a little bit of Barbie.com?
Everybody's running, but not
At the same time, Mom

Dig a tunnel, that's what we do

Do you like my necklace?
Smushed carrots?

Hide before the hyenas come

How to be on the Level

Chet, we are all going to the cabin this weekend,
Can you bring the fam up? sh ya check out
My newPharmasySite

What I say reflects a sensibility
That is more and more widely shared
Without learning what the mind
Has done and tried to do

Because of a certain mental habit
Abandoned in Italy
Social environment doesn't determine
Its significance
The spirit of opposition
Aware of its perpetual change
Can exclude the shadow of suspicion
Go back to your business

Make yourself entirely pure

Watch them suffer

The Editors of Garbage

UGI2ZjRmaGUxd0luRzRBREFCUFg5YTJ2aU5xVXVrNkJOZFJLV0N-
qbkhKL0FkDQp6VzFQWkVTUE0vaHpMcVE4WXp3M1lMUnhmTH-
VBNzhuL0FPdCtGZXJlTkFwOE9YRHVRQUY1SnJtZmh6ck5sZnhyS2-
0zemlUdlQNCnVwNzEwL2l0RnZOTWx0aTIxR0hMVmZVbm9mR2Z-
4VjhXTE1HMGpTNHlrT0FKaU1qYW8vNVpqMlBVK3ZBOWE4en-
RyMjdXQTI5bQ0Kcm5keHRWYy9qajFyMlQ0c2VCenBzTnhlMktiZ0cz-
T1FQOGVUOWE4Mmk4UWZaTlBFRmphcEUrUDNtRGdNZmNqbGor-
Vk51N3VLDQoxaktUUjlVY0Y1WVRHL2RwWEFQK05XNDlLdmR1eD-
BWbXhrTXJaclBrMXJVSG1NanprSE9RcWdLQlU4ZmlPL2FUSW0ya2-
Roay8NCnpOQ3NNRmluaTRLbko2OGRLMnRQWm96aGVXUGNqcFd-
CRnF0MUhlR1I1RDVnT1NEM3F4RmZ1ek02NEE2a0NsWUV6djdReGV-
VTQ0KNElQYyt0Ym1uMm1Cbk9TM1ROY3A0Wkt6cUpIWWZLTXFD-
ZTlkZFlYS3p6K1doNUhjZEt5YU5rWlBpblFEY1FlZEVNTW96

I hear the sound of god whispering in my head

You need something else
More than 40 percent of the 2,749
Never been identified

Tiny fragments to recognizable bones
from skulls, torsos, feet and hands. Some
as large as whole arm and leg bones

To be able to understand oneself
In relation to others
Helped or hindered, enriched
Or impoverished
The palpable need to understand
Our own patch

An EXTRA Six Ounces of Blue Ribbon Award-Winning

Mind your own business
Forever

Just park anywhere

Its swiftness is being renewed
An unnatural bundle
Of splendid creation the real
Audience of rearrangement
Curdles, curdles
And the dogs follow it

Whoa

My name is Penelope
It was impossible to independently verify
The death toll
At the asymmetric battle site

Does it have to be that much?

A weaver of cunning
Whose like-mindedness
is hard to decipher?

Who didn't usurp anyone's place

Comforter

The ruined Prince of the West
In skull orchards and blood singing himself hoarse
The goddamn hurt in his heart
Three years in dreamy slow motion
And supplies approaching "zero"
Stops believing in the possibility
Of a happy workplace
Smiles at the complex locutions
Required to do so

In order to keep the characters straight
One embraces the absence
Acknowledges the verisimilar
Portrayal of genuinely heartless
American assholes
The validity of the endeavor con-
Firmed

When I told You

That I do not let people die on me,
I meant it. I meant it

People die on me

Do not let that die on me
It meant that I
Do not mean when I old
You told people die
On me, meant people do not let
You die I meant

Since I have a memory
There's a lot of blood
It becomes small and helpless
Those men who do not yet feel it
Please don't hold that against me
Still act as though it is normal
A rite of passage of our longing
To be beautiful, our quest
To be men as a going over
To the other side

They even give you cigarettes
As public amusements

By the power invested by ego
I can see the anticipation of effect

I can't make a fist

Great Big Holes of Nothing

It had better be something evil
An A+ instead of an A-

So, you're an A student?

This whole B thang seems to work with you

Oh no, here comes another breeze

I've got to beef up my extra-curriculum

This family is all super-heroes

A "chat" will become a "short talk" and
A "cabin" will be renamed a "small room"

I didn't escape; I came to save my children

The preservation
No where

The Sky Falling Down

Come over here

Oh honey, daddy will take care of you

Stay there, hide
Would you like some more candy?

He's sleeping
No, he's dead

I'm going to push you off the bed

Don't worry

He'll acknowledge you
By and by

Acknowledgements

Appreciation and love to Ruth Danon for entrusting me with the lines "All that's left, he said, is to grow some skin / Skin grows one millimeter a week" culled from an email exchange January 2006 regarding her surgeon, and which lines appear in her own *Code Blue*. Indebtedness and love to Beverly Dahlen for reminding me "don't forget to breathe" the spring following my father's death; and to Kass Fleisher for sharing critical words on neo-feminist rhetoric that I have woven into the poem "Billy Dale Shoots to Kill." Thanks also to Kass and Joe Amato for their constant encouragement to stick to my guns and for helping me to toss the unnecessary.

I would also like to acknowledge and extend gratitude to Jonathon Wilcke, editor of Kootenay School of Writing's *W* 12 "All Music" issue, for publishing a large number of the short poems; to Thom Donovan for granting me the privilege of reading "Billy Dale Shoots to Kill" in the Peace on A series in NYC fall 2006, and for publishing an introduction to and excerpts of the poems on *Wild Horses of Power*; and to Amy King for posting several pieces from the manuscript on *MiPoesias*.

About the Author

Andrew Levy is the author of *Nothing Is in Here* (novella), *Cracking Up, The Big Melt, Memories of My Father, Ashoka, Democracy Assemblages, Values Chauffeur You,* and five other titles of poetry and prose. His poems and essays have appeared in numerous American and international magazines as well as anthologies including *Writing from the New Coast, The Art of Practice: 45 Contemporary Poets, The Gertrude Stein Awards in Innovative American Poetry,* and *Telling It Slant: Avant-Garde Poetics of the 1990s*. He was co-editor with Roberto Harrison and publisher of the poetry journal *Crayon* 1997-2008.

Andrew Levy is a scholar in critical thinking, journalism and creative writing at CUNY's Borough of Manhattan Community College. Prior to his appointment at CUNY, Andrew served as Director of Education Outreach for Columbia University's Nanoscale Science and Engineering Center, and he taught Critical Thinking at NYU's School of Continuing and Professional Studies. Andrew was Affiliate Manager and Special Projects Producer at MediaChannel.org at GlobalVision New Media, Inc. 2000 to 2002. He lives in lower Manhattan with his wife and two daughters.

About Chax Press

Chax Press has been publishing books in Tucson Arizona since 1984. Recent works include books by Norman Fischer, Samuel Ace & Maureen Seaton, Leslie Scalapino, Charles Olson, Mark Weiss, Drum Hadley, fine letterpress chapbooks by Anne Waldman and Eileen Myles, and many more. We have published 139 books to date, and look forward to many more in the next several years. Please visit our web site at chax.org, and look for our books at the Small Press Distribution web site, *http://spdbooks.org*. Chax Press has received support from the Southwestern Foundation for Educational and Historical Preservation, the Tucson Pima Arts Council, the Arizona Commission on the Arts, and the National Endowment for the Arts, but the greatest part of our support comes from individual donors. To join our supporters, please visit our web donation page at *http://chax.org/donate.htm*.

TUCSON PIMA ARTS COUNCIL

Arizona Commission on the Arts

NATIONAL ENDOWMENT FOR THE ARTS